Praise for Shaded Pergola

"*Shaded Pergola* is an exemplary collection of vividly descriptive English-language haiku and original illustrations. Eleni Traganas does not shy away from employing the traditional 5-7-5 syllable format to explore nature's beauty and humanity's complexity in a time when post-modernists strive to throw even the simplest literary rules by the wayside. The crisp images and poignant ponderings invoked by phrases of meticulously chosen words along with exquisitely detailed illustrations showcase the multi-faceted talent Traganas brings to this artfully created masterpiece. *Shaded Pergola* is the ideal specimen every English-language haiku collection should emulate."

— Randal A. Burd, Jr., editor, *Sparks of Calliope*

"Eleni Traganas is a renaissance artist who, being totally self-aware, has mastered the art of conjuring up the infinite and sharing it with us in perfectly formatted haiku. This is not to say that Traganas deals only with abstractions—she doesn't. Her subject matter in *Shaded Pergola* is the everyday, but it is the everyday amplified through her carefully calibrated appreciation. As she says: 'I just see my soul in everyone,' and her vision is absolutely crystal clear! Highly recommended!"

— Ron Kolm, contributing editor, *Sensitive Skin Magazine,* author of *Night Shift* and *Swimming in the Shallow End*

"In this meditative collection, artwork and haiku meet to form a reading experience reminiscent of Basho and the poetry of the T'ang Dynasty. Readers travel the seasons, where newly born crocuses yawn, and hares hide in lettuce patches. Just as spring and summer transition into autumn and winter, so do the verses in this book, all while reminding readers of the intricate beauty nature offers those who look closely. Graceful, like a quiet call to prayer, this collection carefully balances human reflection with lessons from nature. The speaker's keenly observant and carefully revealed feelings form a foundation of trust with readers. Like 'falling autumn leaves,' the haiku offerings sweep readers deeper into their secret places and ask them to look at the world from a more peaceful perspective. This collection attentively blends art and verse to form a unique journey into the quietness the chaotic world too frequently overshadows."

— Nicole Yurcaba, *The US Review of Books*

"Eleni Traganas is an accomplished artist in many fields: musician, composer, painter, pen-and-ink artist, writer, and poet. For the reader, Traganas' *Shaded Pergola* contains an abundance of vividly expressed poems. She has an Asian sensitivity to the minutia of human experiences, of nature, and of seasons. Her collection of poems is an honorable homage to that Japanese and Chinese sensibility."

— Thomas H. Chockley, author of *Personal Myths: Born in Mystery*

SHADED PERGOLA

HAIKU & OTHER SHORT POEMS
With ILLUSTRATIONS

ELENI TRAGANAS

TROPAEUM PRESS

Tropæum Press™
New York

Shaded Pergola: Haiku & Other Short Poems
With Illustrations © Eleni Traganas, 2021, 2022

Poems in this volume were first published in CICADA,
THE AUROREAN, and SACRED JOURNEY

Printed in the United States of America
ISBN: 978-0-578-31198-2

www.elenitraganas.com

To eliminate decrepitude
study the absolute

— Wang Wei
(701-761 AD)

Contents

Long ago on a blisteringly hot July afternoon, I trekked home from the local library under the blazing sun with a cache of books crammed into my tote bag. Scraping a folding chair under the cool shade of the garden pergola thickly overhung with twisting grapevines, I made myself comfortable and excitedly unpacked the volumes that would be accompanying me on my lengthy summer vacation. To a fourteen-year-old bibliophile, every book I examined and lovingly flipped through elicited a fresh and thrilling tactile sensation of great expectations to come: idyllic pastoral poetry, a weighty tome of breathtaking antique engravings, some plant identification guides. And finally, two slim volumes: one modest little grey book of Japanese haiku, and *The White Pony*, a thin paperback book of Chinese poems.

Something intriguing about the misty otherworldly painting on the cover drew me to the latter. Randomly, I opened a page and glanced at a short poem by Wang Wei, poet, painter, and musician of the ancient T'ang period: "The cold mountain turns dark green / The autumn stream flows murmuring on."

These unassuming words instantly elicited a spontaneous synesthetic response: I sensed a shiver of recognition and suddenly felt chilled to the bone, lost in the forlorn icy wilderness of a damp autumnal evening. I shut the book and looked up. The sweltering afternoon heat was building up and intensifying, but my body was oddly immune to the onslaught. Fluffy cumulus clouds were flitting by forming interlocking patterns in the dazzling blue sky as if reaching out to welcome me with open arms into a new, enchanting world. The flowers in the backyard garden seemed to emerge with hues brighter than I recalled: snapdragons, zinnias, geraniums, salvias suddenly grew larger than life in my mind's eye and assumed an immediacy and presence that now magnified and elevated them into a beatified timeless realm that resonated like an internal sounding board. Soon, the saccharine fragrance of a nearby mimosa tree began to bloom into the foreground merging with a rising crescendo of symphonic sounds: stridulating katydids, chirruping sparrows, the neighbor's cat stretching in the dense foliage, the silver pods of a lunaria money plant rustling in the mild breeze. I sat entranced for a few moments, briefly focusing on a solitary leafhopper that was darting from petal to petal on a twining vine, and felt myself merging with the petal, viewing the surrounding world from the vantage point of that tiny, humble insect.

And then, arbitrarily, I opened a page in the little grey book of haiku, my eyes resting on a poem by Gonsui: "Roaring winter storm / Rushing to its utter end... / Ever-sounding sea."

It was July. The notorious New York City heat was oppressive and stultifying. And yet...I thought I could actually hear the howling of savage winds and the cold winter night sweeping me away into a desolate state of death and decay. I closed the little volume. How sad, I thought. And also, how exhilarating! On that singular afternoon many decades ago, I was baptized into the mesmerizing world of haiku.

The haiku and senryu of *Shaded Pergola* were recently composed during the sultry dog days of summer and revisit those first moments of intense discovery. Unlike haiku per se, the occasional examples of the senryu form contained herein deal more specifically with the imperfections of human nature. Although not an essential prerequisite, both forms follow the traditional seventeen-syllable format and were organically conceived with distinct titles, uncharacteristic in haiku craft, yet in this case, an inseparable and integral part of every poem. Along with the natural passage of the seasons, not all imagery is rosy and Arcadian. Vermin, particularly that nemesis of all gardeners and anthophiles, the *Rattus norvegicus*, figure prominently in the narrative, at times disturbing the bucolic aesthetic.

The reverence for tea is evident throughout. This near-mystical potion that purifies, cleanses, and accompanies us in our contemplative sojourn through life, reflects the shifting nature of the seasons like a potent celebration of impermanence, change—and ultimately, transformation.

The short poems included in this collection were composed in response to seemingly quotidian moments that awakened microbursts of fleeting emotions and keenly felt observations. *September Haiku*, for instance, was conceived during a workaday subway trek in Manhattan on a crisp autumn afternoon many years ago. *Autumn-Call*, on the other hand, voices an enduring fascination and respect for that grey-haired Chinese poet and artist who found such solace in his secluded mountain retreat. With original sketches and botanical illustrations inspired by antiquarian engravings, these poems embody evanescent impressions meant to speak for themselves—and lead the reader into a transitory world where nature and the human soul find a common but rarefied affinity.

Shaded

Pergola

Spring

Quickening

From hidden caverns
green lips part the earth: yawning
newly-born crocus

Fair Maidens

Porcelain tears melt
unnoticed on the icy
ground: bashful snowdrops

Consecration

Pink halos surround
the morning peach tree blossoms:
diaphanous wings

Unveiling

My spade rends the earth
in two; under gnarling roots
a naked worm arcs

The Arrival

From the birch copse a
turtle emerges, shaking
off winter boredom

Revival

A letter arrives
from an old friend abroad—the
fragrance of salt air

Love Letter

I open your note
and out flitter purple moths...
just pressed violets

Kismet

My scissors cut deep.
Screaming in pain, the shrub rose
stabs me with its thorn

13

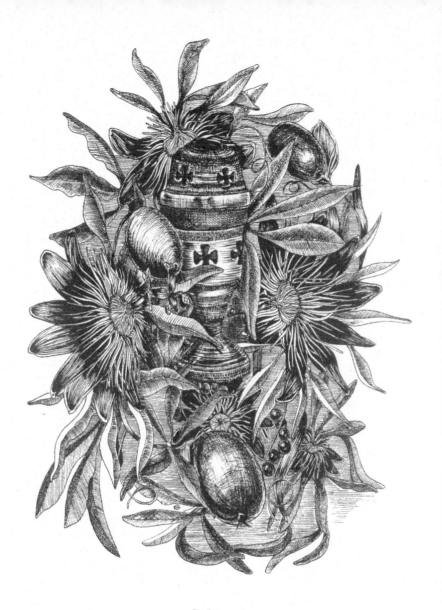

Meditation

Flower of Passion—
soaring on tufts of incense
a crowned head of thorns

Promise

From the somber depths of March
a snowy white owl
shifts in its cradle

Renewal

In the early dawn
cranes bathe in the pond washing
off their nakedness

Green Light

Afternoon rainfall subsides.
Soon, the chirping of
a fearless sparrow

Lordly Cardinal
surveying his terrain: a
silk-robed potentate

Divine Presence

One thing is certain:
throughout my life I have
always heard birds speaking

Ancestors

Generations of
warblers on an ancient tree
singing paeans to God

The Return

Sharp scissors clip the
sky into V-shaped doilies—
tree swallows are back!

Eavesdropping

Nightingales sing on
a telephone pole—we stop
our chat to listen

Pastry Shop

Bright lemon icing
on spongy lime-green cakelets:
spring forsythias!

Garlands

Ambrosial springtime—
soft sugar sweetmeats
decorate the fresh meadows

Envy

Bleeding heart, why do you weep?
Is it that the rose
will soon outshine you?

Colloquium

Frilly flounced parrot tulips
chatter loudly
in the bold April sun

Playtime

Innocence and joy
a sea of smiling faces:
fair yellow pansies

Whirligigs

Maple samaras
sticking on noses—little
children having fun

Confetti

Pale quaking aspens
dusting the landscape
with silvery powder puffs

Boardwalk

After the rainfall
patches of moisture shade the
earthworm's promenade

Skulker

Indolent Maytime—
a quick-witted hare lies low
in the lettuce patch

Raiment

A young girl buttons
her green and pink coat...I dream
of forest sunsets

Recital

Wild oregano and sage
stir the mountains with
ballads of nature

Transformation

Baptized in water
a pure baby-pink
lotus halo emerges

Canticle

Pink break of dawn—
early carnations and
song thrushes crooning duets

Joy

The peal of high-pitched
laughter from the nursery—
sunny sweet williams

Looking Glass

Waiting for an earth
shattering event...meanwhile,
peach blossoms unfold

24

The here and the now:
to a flower, there is
nothing else that matters

High Tea

Plashing spring water
glides over opalescent
pebbles like smooth jade

Sorcery

Wise Solomon's seal
nodding deep in the woodland—
verdant talisman

Child's Play

Prancing in the field...
posies of buttercups and
yellow-chinned moppets

Dowry

Tall cedars line the
climbing mountain road: keys to
the secret hope chest

Walking By Faith

Steep mountain climber,
your heavy backpack poised on
stalwart ant shoulders

New Chapter

Dog-eared pages—
a good night's sleep marks clear lines
of demarcation

Summer

Town Crier

Honey scented air...
a linden tree announces
the dawn of summer

Mystic Tiara

Orange creamsicles
blending with pale pink-blue pearls...
a summer sunset

Silken Gloves

A wisp of cool air
descends upon the garden
like a baby's breath

Rhapsody

Orange tea rose, your
heady fragrance fills my cup
with limpid ardor

Spark Of Dew

"Don't think," says the rose
to the poet. "Thoughts drift
like dandelion fluff"

Hara-Kiri

Pink rosebud bruised and
impaled on a spiky thorn:
honorable death

Carnage

Spots of blood stain the pavement...
a clumsy boot
trampling on rose petals

A Prayer

Sing, bright lark, the sighing
of the human heart, and soar
like incense skywards

Elevation

Gazing upward, she
counts the shifting cumulus clouds
thankful for friends

The Gift

A lifetime searching
for my kindred soul: Look...a
butterfly alights!

Breath Of Life

Sitting still under
the pergola...a summer
breeze rustles my book

Blue Delft

Saturday morning
fresh buttered rolls, a crock of
jam—and an iris

Idler

Late lethargic June—
a red strawberry lounges
on the tablecloth

Summer Dessert

Candied confection
of pink powdered sugar: the
mimosa has bloomed

Pageant

Japanese pagoda tree—
flouncy bridal gown
sprinkling wedding dust

Plunder

Red-mouthed squirrels touching
up their lipstick: scarlet
salvias for dinner

Remains Of The Day

Under the canopy
of peonies, a starling
culls wilted blooms

Launch Pad

Towering rockets
shooting into space...larkspur
and delphinium

Symphony

Ranks of organ pipes
lining the sky—clouds foretell
an evening downpour

Oracle

Low brackish green clouds
thick with oily salt air...
a monster storm brewing

Deluge

Eddying water
swirling higher—soon, the grass
shoots will disappear

Searchlight

Bitter ashes cloud
the air like a pall of death:
firecracker flares

Shape-Shifting

Flash of light, empty
space...from my window a gale
toys with peach-tree limbs

Persistence

Hurricane winds break
the clematis vine in two—
steady roots hold firm

In Extremis

Faint rippling puddle—
after the storm a broken
dahlia breathes its last

Haute Couture

Thick, densely-woven
blanket of lamb's wool.
The summer heat wears a coat

Forest Shanty

Broad-beamed shaded hut—
from under the hosta leaves
a tiny vole peers

Surprise

Furtive cockroach, such
shifty eyes—if only you
could see my slipper!

Demolition

Be forewarned, aphids:
the lady bug has arrived
hungry for a meal

Allure

A leafhopper vaults
towards the pinkish-blue twilight
charmed by young sweet peas

Inspection

Glass-green grasshopper—
I see myself reflected
in your wistful eyes

Royal Mantle

Green iridescent
moss cloaks the primrose path like
jeweled beetles' wings

Night Flashes

Indigo velvet
rhinestone scarf drapes the garden:
dancing fireflies!

Acrobats

On the ceiling a
centipede hovers—tonight
I will wear high heels

Preening

A beetle clicking
in the hush of night? Just a
neighbor's nail clipper

Windstorm

Deafening uproar:
sheets of white noise blind the night—
shrieking cicadas!

Wrangler

No sleep tonight; the
full buck moon kicks high and fast
stirring up trouble

Shootout

Juicy seedpods burst
like trigger-happy pistols—
old-fashioned balsam

Totem Pole

A good luck bouquet
feathery cat's paws piled high—
pussy willow branch

45

Siesta

Deep in the jungle
of shaded ivy, a stray
cat sleeps peacefully

Palm-Leaf

Slouching in the heat
with outstretched limbs...a cat's tail
swishes like a fan

Dipsomania

Tumblers of iced tea
and a good book—summertime
is deep in its cups

Mugged

Tangled in a fine
misty spider's web of dew...
dog days of summer

Kennel Club

Angry puppy jowls
yapping on the terrace...a
pot of snapdragons!

Tintinnabulation

Sonorous church bells
brightly pealing over fields...
blue campanulas

Witching Hour

Gardenias ablaze
in silvery fluorescence:
full milk moon tonight

Crane Flower

Bird of Paradise
sailing on your orange boat
towards faraway lands

Baptism

Break of dawn: a sea
of liquid pearls ripples in
the sun—crystal dew

Dry Spell

Sad keening flowers
whimpering like neglected
puppies—drought season

Nocturne

Waves of susurrating
crickets—soft reassuring
song of August

Mirage

A puppy tied to
a lamppost? Oh, my poor eyes!
Just a brown paper bag

Torpor

Driblets of dampness
basting the body like
watermelon syrup

Suspension

Planks of wood shore up the air
for storage. No breathing
today—heat wave

Sultry Day

It's raining—not quite.
Honeysuckle dewdrops cling
to the skin like oil

51

Glorious Daggers

A phalanx of swords
under a white umbrella:
the yucca at rest

Air Traffic

Low-flying jets on
this balmy August evening—
whining mosquitoes

Sunbath

A pimento and
a gourd tanning cheek-to-cheek
in the sizzling sun

Prism

Jets of water spray
parched sunflowers in the heat:
a crystal rainbow

Berceuse

Broad muted noonday—
a plump hazy shadow fills
out the empty space

Pageboy

Gold strands of cornsilk
curled and bleaching in the sun—
a child's wispy locks

Blitheness

Little child swinging
under the beech tree, trusting
the summer breezes

Largesse

Night and day the moon
and sun shower silver and
gold on our footpath

Fulfillment

White peony tea
and a bowl of cherries...life
is sweet with fragrance

Field Of Dreams

Bronze and copper coins
gleaming in the noonday light...
a wealth of sunflowers

Aria

Song lifting skywards,
heavenly trumpet of grace—
morning glory vine

Locket Charm

Twining grapevine: from
your necklace dangle beaded
jewels of milky jade

Marquee

Striking new red tiles
on the roof—scarlet runner
beans are growing fast

Moxie

Abandoned in the
garden, a solitary
rose defies the weeds

Finish Line

Last breath of August:
a leap of color shudders,
sprints…then collapses

Fruition

Musky whiff of air—
ripe September apples in
a cedar barrel

Nectar Of The Gods

Ambrosial gift:
poised on an uppermost branch...
a succulent peach

Flight Of Fancy

Crisp mountain air—my
heady thoughts are transported
to mythical times

Autumn

&

Winter

Final Course

Early pensive fall—
baked smoky apples cool in
the wan candlelight

Coming Of Age

Four juicy pears poised
on a window ledge dreaming
of the great escape

Idyll

Fruit-colored sky
awash in apricot tints—
honeyed taste of autumn

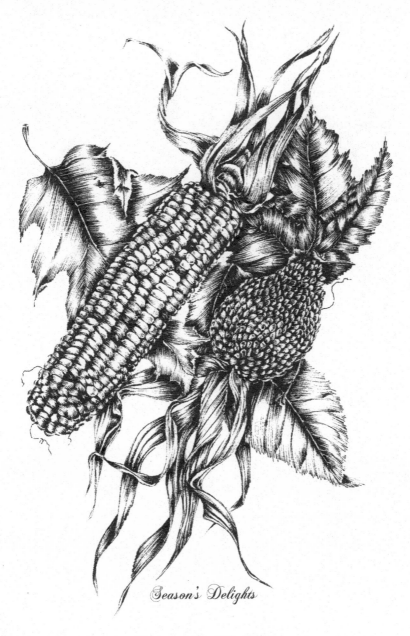

Season's Delights

Glass candy dish filled
with orange toffee comfits—
falling autumn leaves

Skirmish

Yesterday's foxgloves
are now a toppled amusement
park for stray cats

Haunted Spot

Soft panting sparrow—
your seed-like eyes speak volumes;
soon the rats shall feast

Standoff

Staring at me, the
rat holds his ground, then retreats
into his burrow

Unveiled

Subdued evenfall—
a hooded crow flies away
betrayed by the moon

Magick

Deep in the larch grove
a fairy ring of mushrooms
rollicks in moonlight

After Dark

Shrill noises at night:
raccoons screech, a rat barks—I
shut my window tight

The Gloaming

Spectral ghosts haunt the
moonlit dusk...white bed sheets
twisting on a clothesline

Closure

Spindly knotted weeds
tumble sparsely in the wind—
scattered autumn hopes

Memento Mori

Stray feathers rest on
a mound of dry leaves...a pair
of cat's eyes glimmers

Armistice

Black and white flag of
truce flapping on a rusty
fence: ambushed raccoon

Hierarchy

A bird, a rat, and
a stray cat—the king's pecking
order reigns supreme

Conspiracy

Pitter-patter of
rainfall in the dead of night?
Just rats whispering

Trapped

Searching upwards with
doleful eyes, a baby rat
surrenders its fate

Resignation

Mourning doves huddle
mutely under the eaves, grieved
by the falling rain

Two-Faced

How the cherry tree
develops over time:
one year sweet—then sour

Wrong Turn

A knotted stub on
the old oak tree trunk: a friend
stumbles on their path

Bitter Wine

Raw hops and barbed twigs
laced with vinegar:
a friendship cup turned sour

Hourglass

Stone angels mark time
in the graveyard while daylilies
shed their petals

Postlude

Languid November—
a slender rusty twig naps
in a pewter cup

Provenance

Old antique piano
once a slumbering bud in
the northern pine woods

Demise

Crumbling pergola
now rotting wood not even
fit for a pencil

Survivor

Cold lips numb with death:
only the chrysanthemum's
voice speaks in autumn

Changing Guard

Scratchy nib of my
empty fountain pen—the world
is slipping away

Blocked

Don't beat the dumb beast—
his thoughts are slow to come. Ah!
My blank manuscript...

Lifeline

Chafed hands in tweed woolen
coat pockets reach for the
last crumbs of shortbread

Eye-to-Eye

"You're so kind," he says.
"I just see my soul
in everyone," she replies

Contentment

Only fools pity
an old man living alone
with his cup of tea

Sleepless again. Off
to the kitchen for a cup
of tea...and a cat

Great Expectations

After a restless night,
a plateful of poached eggs...
and molten sunrise

Old hag beating rugs
echoes thunder through the cliffs—
snowflakes spray like dust

Wizening

Beneath the bare oak tree
gnarled calloused hands rake leaves—
a rook stealing twigs

Homeward

Harsh January—
Through the steamy windowpane
a warm tea kettle

Poetaster

Bright orange sunset:
if only I could pour you
in my cup like tea...

Celebration

Streams of ice-laced air
wrap the night like silk ribbons...
unexpected gift!

Tinsel

Bare February—
a shredded ornament hangs
from an icy branch

Abdication

Paper lanterns sway
like fragile marble castles.
The wasp queens have gone

Cadenza

Ear-splitting brass trumpet
shocking the air—the
amaryllis has bloomed!

Bottom Line

One final patch of
sunlight slicing the sky like
a dull paring knife

Absolution

Thoughts after thoughts piled
high in bundles ready for
winter firewood

Anticipation

Icy wintertime—
a shovel clears the way for
tomorrow's picnic

Christmas Rose

Blooming in a cold
and shaded mound: Look!
Hope in the dead of winter

Stern Reaper

Forbidden hallway—
old grandfather clock waves his
hand reproachfully

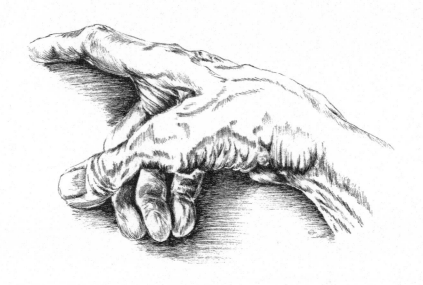

Timeline

Thin stalks withering
fragile as a hollow straw—
old age approaches

Illusion

Melting icicles
in the glassy gold sunset:
fleeting dreams of spring

Gestation

Submerged in frost rime
a pergola of spring hopes
silently quickens

Swan Song

A crisp leaf dances
joyfully on its stalk, glad
to have been alive

Short Poems

September Haiku

Blankets hang and sway:
the scent of camphor vapors
cools the autumn air

Gladioli stir
a crickets' chorus chirping...
counterpoint of sounds

Morning glory seeds
glisten in the azure sky...
graceful jeweled earrings

Digging garden bulbs
damp with must and loamy soil—
squirrels fluff out their tails

Crackling cones of pine
sparkle in the fireplace—
scented spiced mulled wine

Curlicues of steam
floating upwards from my breath...
crisp the tea-red road

Doors are barred and shut,
flames dance on the gas-lit stove—
fragrant pumpkin pies

Ears so cold, my cat!
Behind storm windows you stare
at the parting clouds

Shadows stretch and yawn
a slanting sun sinks deeper...
tombstones rise and fall

Winter Haiku

Barking winds rage by
like angry dogs. These winter
days have no manners!

Footprints near the door
a brass knocker cloaked in snow...
just a strolling cat

Two stems of freesias
huddling close in a glass vase...
the chill air lingers

The lilt of snoring
at the crack of dawn? A distant
shovel scraping snow

Scuttling inside for warmth
like all the rest of us,
poor, pitiful roach!

That fragrance: a pine
forest, thyme honey? Or
my cedar hope chest...

Crinkling raindrops tap
and dance on metal awnings—
blackbirds hush their song

Tossed in the gutter
with stale hambones and fruit peels...
an old Christmas tree

The crunch of tires
on a crooked asphalt road...
meandering thoughts

Stark widow's fingers
knitting a long, fringed mantle—
bony icicles!

The full moon trembles
like a copper gong in the
symphony of night

Three Short Poems

Bitter Gall

We pour our thoughts
through a wide-mouthed funnel.
Into a cup they drop
and curdle like resinous cheese.

A sieve would have been
the better tool.

Epitaph

Death:
Bereft of
Breath.

Mute:
Broken flute.

Hollow tube:
Soul sucked
Through.

Grief:
Disbelief.

Sense, thought:
Naught

Illusion

Yellow is too hot a color
to wear—blinding the sun
like a tropical budgerigar
electric lights flashing on
and off even in the clash
and noise of daylight. Bright
and showy plumage, the apple
of our caged and restless eye.

This summer flew by
like a chattering bird.
My Youth.

Soliloquy

What shall we pray for
facing east each dawn
before the sun our shrine:
For wealth and riches,
to our health? Or merely

to catch a shaft of Light
within our eyes...

Autumn-Call

Geranium on the window yellows
as the sun removes its glow.
A crusted leaf escapes the storm wind
through the open door. Corners
of the room turn cold as palms
stretch out upon the wall.

Old Wang Wei sits within, his autumn hair
reflected in the cups of tea, chrysanthemum
and marigold, chipped crockery,
his wife, alone, where no one treads
the mossy damp and twisted bracken rusted brown.

Pain grips the throat.   The gate shuts tight.
New seeds like scattered on the ground.